PRACTICAL COOKERY GUIDE BOOK FOR PARENTS AND SCHOOL TEACHERS

DR ANSHUMALI PANDEY | CHEF PARESH FULBARIA

Made with ♥ on the Notion Press Platform
www.notionpress.com

This book is dedicated to all the educators, parents, and caregivers who are passionate about teaching children how to cook. Your dedication to providing hands-on cooking experiences for children helps them develop life-long skills and encourages healthy eating habits.

We also dedicate this book to the children who participated in cooking classes and shared their enthusiasm and love for learning about food. You are the inspiration for this book and we hope it will continue to inspire many more children to discover the joy of cooking.

Contents

Contents

Preface

Cooking with children is a joyful and educational experience that can inspire curiosity, creativity, and a love for healthy and delicious food. As children participate in the kitchen, they not only develop practical cooking skills but also enhance their literacy, numeracy, science, and social-emotional abilities. Cooking can also be a way to explore different cultures, traditions, and values, and to connect with others through food.

However, cooking with children can also present challenges and risks if not done properly. Teachers, parents, and caregivers need to be aware of food safety, hygiene, nutrition, and developmental appropriateness when planning and conducting cooking activities with children. They also need to consider the resources, equipment, and materials available, as well as the cultural, social, and economic backgrounds of the children and families involved.

This book aims to provide practical and evidence-based guidance on how to cook with children in a safe, fun, and meaningful way. It is based on the personal and long experience of the author Dr Anshumali Pandey and various users, who shared their experiences, insights, and questions about cooking with children. The book is organized into chapters that cover different aspects of cooking with children, such as planning, preparation, safety, equipment, recipes, and cultural diversity. Each chapter includes practical tips, examples, and suggestions based on the chat conversations, as well as additional resources and references for further learning.

The book is intended for teachers, parents, and caregivers who want to engage children in cooking activities, as well as for students, researchers, and practitioners in the fields of education, nutrition, and child development. It is not a comprehensive guide or a cookbook, but rather a collection of ideas and experiences that can inspire and inform cooking with children.

We hope that this book will encourage more people to cook with children and to discover the joys and benefits of this rewarding activity. We also hope that it will spark further conversations and collaborations among educators, parents, and researchers, and contribute to a more inclusive, healthy, and sustainable food culture for all.

Prologue

Hello There!

As a self trained pediatrician and a long serving Trainer Chef, I have seen firsthand the impact that healthy eating habits can have on a child's growth and development. As a parent myself, I know how challenging it can be to encourage children to try new foods and engage in cooking activities.

That's why I'm thrilled to introduce this book, which is based on a conversation about cooking with children. The conversation includes valuable tips and insights from experts in the field of nutrition, education, and child development.

In this book, we'll explore the benefits of cooking with children, how to set up a successful cooking class, age-appropriate skills and equipment, and tips for keeping children safe in the kitchen. We'll also provide examples of simple and healthy recipes that you can make with your children, and discuss how to make cooking relevant to classroom projects and cultural diversity.

Whether you are a teacher, a parent, or a caregiver, this book will provide you with practical and effective strategies for making cooking a fun and educational experience for children. So let's get cooking!

Dr Anshumali Pandey

CHAPTER ONE

Make Connections

This book provides detailed guidance for teachers who are planning a cooking class for their students. It highlights the importance of connecting the cooking class to the existing curriculum components and suggests various strategies for achieving this goal.

The first step in planning a cooking class is to ask yourself what curriculum components you would like to cover. This will help you design a cooking class that complements and enhances the lessons you are already teaching in the classroom.

Cooking in the classroom is only sustainable when it directly connects to the lessons you are already teaching. Therefore, it is essential to plan the cooking class in a way that complements and enhances the existing curriculum components.

To make the cooking class more successful, you are suggested introducing information about the cooking class or its ingredients ahead of time. This can help generate interest and curiosity among the students, and it can also help them understand the origin and nutritional value of the ingredients they will be using in the cooking class. For instance, I recommend reading a children's book about an ingredient and how it is grown.

Additionally, I suggest referring to standardized recipes for ideas on journal assignments linked to cooking classes. This approach can help students learn more about the recipe's ingredients and their nutritional value, and it can also encourage them to write about their cooking experiences.

If collaborating with a chef, I recommend establishing good communication and sharing ideas. It is important to talk with the chef about your expectations and goals for the cooking experience and gather the information you need to introduce the recipe and its ingredients ahead of time. This can help ensure that the chef's expertise and the teacher's objectives are aligned, resulting in a successful and enjoyable cooking class for the students.

The importance of connecting the cooking class to the existing curriculum components, introducing information about the cooking class or its ingredients ahead of time, and collaborating effectively with a chef to achieve the desired objectives cannot be more emphasized.

CHAPTER TWO

Plan and Prepare

When planning a cooking class, one of the critical factors to consider is selecting a recipe that includes fresh ingredients that are easily accessible to both the teacher and the students. Using fresh ingredients not only makes the recipe healthier but also allows the students to learn about the different types of produce available in their area.

Another essential aspect of planning a cooking class is breaking down the recipe into clear and manageable steps. The teacher should carefully consider the age group they are instructing and ensure that the steps are appropriate for their skill level. It is also essential to identify activities that the children can do themselves, hands-on, throughout the process. This approach helps keep the children engaged and encourages them to take an active role in the cooking process.

Additionally, the teacher should determine what supplies will be needed for each step and gather and organize those tools ahead of time. This can include pots, pans, measuring cups, spoons, and any other kitchen utensils required for the recipe. It is crucial to ensure that there are enough supplies available for each child to participate fully in the cooking class.

Depending on the age group of the students and the time available for the cooking class, the teacher may need to ask a volunteer or parent to prep some ingredients ahead of time. For instance, younger children may require more assistance with chopping or measuring ingredients, whereas older children may be able to handle these tasks independently. In any case, it is essential to plan ahead and ensure that the necessary preparations have been made before the cooking class begins.

In conclusion, when planning a cooking class, the teacher should consider factors such as ingredient availability, age-appropriate steps, hands-on activities, required supplies, and necessary preparations. By carefully considering these elements, the teacher can create a fun and engaging cooking experience for the students, which can help them develop important life skills such as healthy eating habits and kitchen safety.

CHAPTER THREE

Helping Hands

When planning a cooking class, it can be helpful to ask parents or guardians to come in and help with the instruction. However, it is not always possible for parents to volunteer their time. In such cases, the teacher can turn to other resources in the community, such as local clubs and organizations.

Many community groups, such as local clubs, church groups, and Lions clubs, focus on helping in schools and are often eager to find volunteer opportunities. These organizations can be an excellent resource for finding volunteers to assist with cooking classes. Teachers can reach out to these organizations to see if they have any volunteers available to help with the class.

Another great resource for finding volunteers is local colleges and universities. Many schools have service learning offices that can connect teachers with college students looking for volunteer opportunities. These students can be a valuable resource for teachers, as they often have experience working with children and can provide extra support during cooking classes.

When planning hands-on activities in the classroom, having extra people to help with set up, supervision, and clean up is crucial. Volunteers can help with tasks such as setting up workstations, supervising the students as they work, and cleaning up afterward. By having extra help, teachers can ensure that the cooking class runs smoothly and that all of the students are able to participate fully in the activities.

In conclusion, when planning a cooking class, teachers should consider asking parents, community groups, colleges, or other resources for volunteers to assist with the instruction. By having extra people to help with set up, supervision, and clean up, teachers can create a safe and engaging environment for the students to learn and develop important life skills.

CHAPTER FOUR

Prepare a Back-Up Activity

When teaching a cooking class, there are often moments when students may have to wait for the next step in the process. Whether it is waiting for the dish to cook or waiting for other groups to finish their assigned tasks, it is essential to have activities planned to keep the students engaged and focused on the lesson.

One way to fill this waiting time is to plan an activity related to the recipe being prepared. For example, if the students are preparing a salad, you could provide them with worksheets featuring a big empty bowl and ask them to draw the vegetables and ingredients they would add to their salads. This activity not only keeps the students engaged but also helps them to think creatively about their choices of ingredients and how they can customize their salads.

Another idea is to bring children's books related to the recipe and ask the students to illustrate the steps of the recipe. This activity not only reinforces the steps of the recipe but also develops the students' literacy skills and creativity.

Another option is to provide students with journal topics related to the recipe or the ingredients. For instance, you could ask them to write about their favorite vegetable or to reflect on their experience cooking with a particular ingredient. Journaling is an excellent way to encourage reflection, creativity, and critical thinking, and can help students develop their writing skills.

Overall, it is essential to have activities planned to keep students engaged during any waiting periods in the cooking process. By planning activities that are related to the recipe or ingredients, teachers can ensure that students are learning and having fun while they wait for the next step in the cooking process. By incorporating different activities, teachers can create a comprehensive and engaging cooking class that enhances students' learning experience.

CHAPTER FIVE

Practice at Home

Before teaching a cooking class to a group of children, it is essential to prepare and test the recipe beforehand. I recommend cooking the dish at home on your own or with your children or grandchildren to gain an understanding of the recipe and what aspects of the project students may need guidance with.

By testing the recipe, you can identify any potential challenges that the students may face and plan ahead to address them. For instance, you may find that certain steps in the recipe are too complex or require advanced cooking techniques, which may be difficult for younger students to master. In this case, you can plan to provide extra guidance or instruction to help them understand the process better.

Additionally, as you prepare the recipe, it is essential to think about how to adapt it to children, what their challenges might be, and how to refine the instructions to fit the age level and abilities of the students. This may involve simplifying the recipe, breaking it down into smaller steps, or using visuals or demonstrations to help students understand the process better.

By testing the recipe ahead of time, you can also identify any potential safety hazards and plan ahead to prevent accidents. For instance, you may need to ensure that students are using appropriate kitchen tools and equipment, and that they are using them safely and correctly.

Overall, testing the recipe before teaching a cooking class to a group of children is an essential step in the preparation process. It helps teachers to identify potential challenges and safety hazards, refine the instructions, and plan ahead to ensure that the students have a safe and enjoyable cooking experience.

CHAPTER SIX

Clear Communication

Clear and concise instructions are crucial for any successful cooking class. As a teacher, it's important to plan ahead and break down the recipe into clear and concise steps that students can easily follow. Before teaching the class, it's recommended to practice communicating those steps out loud to ensure that they are easily understood.

As you plan and make a sample of your recipe, it's important to note the key steps and identify any potential challenges that students may face. For instance, you may need to simplify certain steps or provide additional instructions to help students understand the process better.

Being able to recognize and simplify the steps of a recipe is a vital component of a successful cooking class. This involves breaking down the recipe into smaller steps, using simple language, and providing clear and concise instructions. It's important to keep in mind that students may have varying levels of experience in the kitchen, so it's essential to tailor the instructions to fit their abilities. In addition to clear and concise steps, it's also important to provide students with visuals, demonstrations, and hands-on practice to help them understand the recipe better. For instance, you may want to show students how to chop vegetables or demonstrate how to mix ingredients together.

Clear and concise steps are key to a successful cooking class. As a teacher, it's essential to plan ahead, practice communicating the steps out loud, and identify potential challenges to ensure that students have a safe and enjoyable cooking experience. By breaking down the recipe into smaller steps, using simple language, and providing clear instructions, students will be able to follow along easily and gain a better understanding of the cooking process.

Use Appropriate Vocabulary

Using appropriate vocabulary is important when teaching children how to cook. It is essential to explain the steps of the recipe in a way that children can easily understand. Use simple language and avoid using complex words that may confuse or intimidate the students. For example, instead of saying "sauté" or "sear," use words like "cook" or "brown" that are more familiar to children.

Assuming that most students will not be familiar with cooking terms, it is also important to introduce them to new words and concepts in a way that is engaging and informative. When reviewing the recipe, identify one or two cooking terms that may be unfamiliar to the students and provide a clear explanation of those terms during the demonstration. For example, if the recipe calls for "fold in the ingredients," explain what that means and demonstrate it in a way that the students can easily understand.

To help reinforce new vocabulary, you can print out the terms and their definitions to present during the class. This will not only help the students remember the terms but will also serve as a valuable resource for them to refer to later on. By using appropriate vocabulary and introducing new terms in an engaging way, you can help children develop their culinary skills and understanding of cooking concepts.

CHAPTER SEVEN

Feature Local Food

Choosing a recipe that features ingredients you can source locally has multiple benefits. Firstly, it promotes the use of locally grown produce which supports the local economy and reduces carbon footprint associated with transporting food from distant locations. Secondly, it introduces the concept of seasonality and encourages students to try new, fresh ingredients that they may not have encountered before.

To further emphasize the importance of locally sourced ingredients, you can inform your students about the environmental and health benefits of eating locally grown food. You can explain how locally grown produce is often picked when it is ripe, resulting in better taste and nutritional value.

In addition to highlighting the benefits of locally sourced ingredients, it's also important to inform students where they can purchase such ingredients. You can provide a list of local farmers markets, co-ops, and farm stands that offer fresh, seasonal produce. Sharing information about where to find locally grown ingredients can help students to make more informed choices when grocery shopping and can also increase their awareness of the local food system.

To further educate students about the local food system, you can distribute local food guides, farm profiles, and promotional materials. These materials can include information about local farms and their products, as well as schedules for farmers markets and other events related to locally grown food. By providing these resources, you can encourage students to become more engaged in their local food community and to explore new ways of incorporating locally sourced ingredients into their cooking.

CHAPTER EIGHT

One Step Ahead

Observation and attention to individual needs are essential when instructing a cooking class with children. As students work on their assigned steps, it's important to monitor their progress and anticipate their needs. By doing so, you can provide guidance, encouragement, or assistance when necessary.

One way to stay tuned to the students‘ needs is to move around the classroom, watching and listening to their progress. You can also ask questions to gauge their understanding of the recipe and to encourage critical thinking. By asking open-ended questions, you can prompt them to consider different possibilities and outcomes.

Observation also allows you to identify teachable moments and recurring questions. When you notice a common question or a topic that needs clarification, it's an opportunity to stop the whole class and explain the concept or praise a student's work. For example, if several students are struggling with measuring ingredients accurately, you can pause the class and demonstrate the proper technique, allowing all students to benefit from the teaching.

It is important to give positive feedback to students throughout the class. Praise can help build students' confidence and reinforce their learning. Encourage their creativity and problem-solving skills, and celebrate their successes, both big and small. By giving students the support and guidance they need, they will feel more comfortable and motivated to learn, leading to a successful and enjoyable cooking class experience.

CHAPTER NINE

Answering to every "Why?"

When teaching a cooking class, it is important to not only explain the steps of the recipe, but also to convey the "why" behind the recipe. By doing so, you can spark students' interest and encourage them to participate fully in the cooking process. To achieve this, talk with the students about the ingredients you have chosen, where you bought them from, and the importance of healthy eating.

When selecting a recipe, consider highlighting local and seasonal ingredients that you can source from nearby farms. This will provide an opportunity to discuss the benefits of buying and consuming local produce, such as supporting the local economy, reducing the carbon footprint, and enjoying fresh and flavorful ingredients. You can also provide local food guides and promotional materials, including farm profiles and farmers market schedules, to encourage students and their families to explore local food options.

Sharing the back-story of the recipe can also make the experience more meaningful for students. You might share a personal anecdote about a time when you cooked the same recipe with your family, or talk about a neighbor who gave you the recipe. You can also discuss the farmers who grew the ingredients and what their farms might have looked like. By sharing your enthusiasm for the recipe and how it connects to local food and healthy eating, you can inspire students to try it out in the classroom and to continue cooking at home.

CHAPTER TEN

Recognizing Opportunities for Learning

Introducing new vocabulary, new skills, and new ideas throughout the cooking project can make the class more engaging and educational for students. You can start by selecting a children's book related to the recipe or the ingredients and read it out loud to the students. The book could teach them new vocabulary or concepts related to healthy eating, local food, or cooking techniques.

Another way to introduce new vocabulary is to write key words on the board and explain them as you go along. You can also ask the students to keep a food journal where they can write about their experience cooking and tasting new foods. This journal can also include reflections on the new skills they learned or new ideas they were exposed to during the class.

As you go through the recipe, point out new skills that the students are learning, such as measuring ingredients, cutting vegetables, or sautéing. You can also have them practice these skills on their own or with a partner.

Breaking down the recipe into smaller, more manageable steps can help students build their confidence and feel more comfortable in the kitchen.

Encourage students to share their own ideas and experiences related to the recipe. For example, if you're making a family recipe, ask the students if they have any family recipes that they would like to share. This can help create a sense of community and foster a love for cooking and sharing food.

CHAPTER ELEVEN

Be Understanding and Encouraging

Introducing new foods to children can be a challenge, as children can often be picky eaters. Therefore, it's important to have realistic expectations when introducing new foods to children. It's recommended that a new food should be offered to a child a number of times before they develop a taste for it. Forcing children to eat something they don't want to eat can often backfire and make them even more resistant to trying new foods.

If a child is hesitant to try a new recipe, it's important to create a non-threatening and welcoming environment. Encourage the child to smell the food or ask another student to describe the taste. It's important not to draw attention to a child who doesn't want to try the recipe, as this can make them feel uncomfortable or embarrassed. Instead, gently encourage all students to try just a taste of the new recipe, emphasizing that it's okay if they don't like it.

It's also important to recognize that taste preferences can vary from child to child. Some children may be more adventurous eaters than others. Therefore, it's important to create a positive and encouraging environment that respects each child's individual taste preferences.

Throughout the cooking class, it's a good idea to introduce new vocabulary, skills, and ideas related to healthy eating and cooking. Reading a children's book related to the recipe or developing journal activities can help reinforce these concepts in a fun and engaging way. By providing a well-rounded experience, students are more likely to develop an interest in cooking and healthy eating habits.

CHAPTER TWELVE

Encourage Children to Have Positive Attitudes about Food

- Have a positive attitude toward foods and the mealtime experience. Remember, a negative attitude expressed by adults and children may influence other children to not try that food.
- Introduce new and fun ways to eat vegetables and fruits with creative recipes. When introducing new food to children, serve a small amount of the new food along with more popular and familiar foods.
- Include children in the food activities to encourage them to try new foods and to gain self-confidence.
- Serve finger foods. Foods cut smaller are easier for children to handle.
- Do not force a child to eat. Children often go through food jags. It is normal for a child to ask for second helpings of food one day, yet eat very lightly the next day.

- Provide a comfortable atmosphere at mealtime. Mealtime is also a social activity. Therefore, allow children to talk with others.
- Encourage children to eat food or new foods in a low-key way. For instance, read a book about a new food that will be served that day, and serve the new food at snack time when children are hungrier.
- Introduce a new food five or six times over a few weeks, instead of only once or twice. The more exposure children have to a food, the more familiar and comfortable it becomes and the more likely they will be to try the food.
- Offer the new food to a child who eats most foods. Children usually follow other children and try the food.
- Have staff eat with the children. Have them eat the same foods that have been prepared for the children.
- Do not offer food related bribes or rewards. This only reinforces that certain foods are not desirable.
- Respect refusals.

Caregivers are responsible for:

- What foods are offered
- When foods are offered
- Where foods are offered

Children are responsible for determining:

- What foods they eat
- How much, or even if, they eat

CHAPTER THIRTEEN

Tips for Cooking With Students

- Choose a recipe that includes familiar ingredients the kids and their families can find at any grocery store or tailgate market.
- Feature locally grown products. Tell the children about the farms in their area. Linking food with farms will encourage students to try new things, and will encourage them to make healthy choices.
- Pick a recipe that matches the children's abilities and attention span.
- Print copies of the recipe so students can share it with their parents.
- Break recipes into steps, and be sure you have adequate tools for the number of children in your cooking class. Pictorial recipes are great for younger children.
- Wash your hands before getting started, and ask the students to wash their hands as well. Highlight food safety and proper handling of food and tools throughout the class.
- If the class setup allows, organize "stations" where the kids can complete different steps of the recipe. Organize

the cooking tools by station. Involve the students in the preparation of the recipe.

- Give a quick (and enthusiastic) description of the recipe you will be making. Read the recipe aloud or explain what you will be doing first, second, and so on to prepare the food.
- Show the children the ingredients, and tell them something about the key components of the recipe—which farm you bought it from, why you like to cook with it, why it is good for you, etc.
- Ask the students what they know about farms. You can ask: Has anyone ever been to a farm? What did you see there?
- If you are working with vegetables, hold the vegetables up for everyone to see and identify the part(s) of the plants they will be eating and which parts they will be cutting off and discarding.
- Ask sensory questions like What does this smell like? What does it look like? Does it taste bitter or sweet? Does it feel soft or rough? Especially for younger kids, it is helpful to ask them “either-or” questions instead of open-ended ones.
- Have plenty of ingredients so that all of the kids can participate.

CHAPTER FOURTEEN

Tips for Selecting Recipes for Children

- Are the hands-on skills age/developmentally appropriate? When selecting a recipe for a cooking class, it is important to consider the age and developmental level of the children you will be working with. Choose a recipe that matches their abilities and offers them an opportunity to learn new skills that are appropriate for their age. For younger children, simple tasks like mixing ingredients or spreading butter on bread may be appropriate, while older children may be able to chop vegetables or use kitchen tools like a blender or food processor.
- Do you have access to needed equipment? Before you plan a cooking project, make sure you have access to all the necessary equipment. Depending on the recipe, you may need a stove, oven, blender, food processor, mixing bowls, cutting boards, knives, measuring cups, and spoons. Consider what equipment is available in your classroom, school kitchen, or community center, and plan accordingly.

- Does the recipe connect with children's interests or classroom projects? Choose a recipe that connects with the children's interests or classroom projects. If you are studying a particular region, culture, or historical period, consider choosing a recipe that reflects that focus. If you are working on a unit about healthy eating, select a recipe that promotes nutritious ingredients and balanced meals. If you know that your students love pizza, try making homemade pizza together.
- Does the recipe promote healthy food choices? When selecting a recipe, consider whether it promotes healthy food choices. Look for recipes that feature whole grains, fresh fruits and vegetables, lean protein, and low-fat dairy. Consider substituting less healthy ingredients with healthier alternatives. For example, you can use applesauce instead of oil in baking recipes, or substitute Greek yogurt for sour cream in dips.
- Does the recipe feature seasonal and local products children can find in the garden or on a local farm? Choose a recipe that features seasonal and local products that children can find in the garden or on a local farm. This helps children understand where their food comes from, and encourages them to try new foods. For example, in the fall, you can make pumpkin soup using fresh pumpkin from a local farm, or in the summer, you can make a salad with tomatoes and cucumbers from a nearby garden.
- Is the recipe culturally relevant? Select a recipe that is culturally relevant and reflects the diversity of your students. Consider recipes that represent different cultures, regions, or traditions. This can help build cultural awareness and sensitivity, and foster a sense of community in the classroom.

- Is the recipe affordable for all families, and does it use familiar ingredients they have at home? Finally, choose a recipe that is affordable for all families, and uses ingredients that they may already have at home. Consider using staple ingredients like rice, beans, pasta, or potatoes, which are often inexpensive and can be used in a variety of recipes.

CHAPTER FIFTEEN

Tips for Introducing Recipes to Children

- Prepare a simple recipe chart: Having a recipe chart can help children visualize the recipe steps and understand the sequence of actions needed to complete the recipe. The chart should include a list of ingredients, the amounts needed, and the steps involved in the recipe. You can use pictures or illustrations to help the children understand the recipe steps better. For example, if you are making a salad, you can include pictures of the different vegetables and dressings, and how they are cut or mixed together.
- Have examples of ingredients in their raw form: Before starting the recipe, show children the different ingredients in their raw form so they can identify them and become familiar with them. This can also be an opportunity to talk about the different nutritional benefits of each ingredient and how they contribute to a healthy diet. You can pass around the raw ingredients so children can see, touch, and smell them, and ask them to describe what they notice about each one.

- Read the recipe aloud, discussing each step: It's important to read the recipe aloud to the children, step by step, to ensure they understand each action required to complete the recipe. Encourage children to ask questions if they are unsure about anything, and offer explanations and clarifications as needed. You can also point out any potential challenges or pitfalls in the recipe, and discuss how to overcome them.
- Discuss rules and/or safety considerations and have children identify these for specific steps: Before starting the recipe, review any rules or safety considerations with the children, such as using knives, operating the oven or stove, or handling hot pots or pans. Have children identify the specific steps in the recipe that require caution or careful attention, and reinforce safe practices throughout the cooking process. For example, you can remind children to wash their hands frequently, to use oven mitts or potholders when handling hot items, and to keep the kitchen area clean and organized.

CHAPTER SIXTEEN

Tips for Working with Chefs

- It is important to inform the chef about any food allergies or dietary restrictions in your class ahead of time. This allows the chef to adjust the recipe or provide alternative ingredients that are safe for all students. Additionally, make sure the chef is aware of any knife or open flame policies that your school or classroom follows.
- Confirm the time, location, and date of the cooking demonstration with the chef several days before the event. This ensures that both parties are clear on the details and can make any necessary adjustments.
- Discuss event logistics with the chef. Determine what the class set up will be, where students will be working, and how long the class will last. Make sure to inform the chef of any important activities or events that may be disrupted by their early arrival to set up.
- Brainstorm with the chef how the recipe can connect with aspects of your curriculum and ensure that the children's participation is developmentally appropriate. Discuss how the recipe will be taught and how the

students will be involved in the cooking process.

- Discuss how you will prepare students for the cooking class/demonstration and communicate with the chef about what follow-up will take place after the class. This can include writing reflections or creating a recipe book with the students.
- Ask the chef if they can provide recipes to send home with the children or if there are other recipes that can be cooked in the classroom as a future project.
- Ask the chef if there are any preparations that need to be completed before the cooking class or demonstration. This can include prepping ingredients, setting up equipment, or reviewing safety procedures.
- Plan on assisting the chef during the entire cooking demonstration or class. This can include helping to manage the students and connecting the cooking experience back to their curriculum.
- If possible, recruit a parent or community member to help during the cooking class. Let the chef know how many students will be in the cooking class and how many volunteers will be there to help. Having extra hands can make the experience more enjoyable for everyone involved.

CHAPTER SEVENTEEN

Tips for Working with Teachers

- When setting up a cooking class, ask the teacher if any of the students have food allergies and ask about any knife/open flame policies the school or classroom follows.
- Make sure you are both clear about the time, location, and the date of the cooking demonstration.
- Check in with the teacher several days before the demo.
- Communicate with the teacher about event logistics. What will the class set up be? Will the students be working on desks or tables? How long can the class last? If you arrive early to set up will you be disrupting anything important?
- Ask teachers how students will be prepared for the demonstration and what follow up will take place.
- Experiences are more memorable and meaningful if they build on each other. Ask teachers what they are currently working on in the classroom or if students have recently gone on any field trips to tie your activity into their recent experience. Being able to connect with students on common experience will give you a foot

in the door and remove a one-time cooking class from isolation. If the teacher requests that you connect the cooking demonstration to a particular lesson or study topic and you need support with this, contact ASAP. We have tons of ideas and can help.

- Let teachers know in advance what recipe you are planning so that they have the opportunity to integrate it into their classroom. Children will feel like experts when they arrive to make pumpkin soup if they have been researching pumpkins in the classroom. The broader the experience children have with healthy food, the more impact it will have on their food choices.
- Help teachers with follow up. Give them recipes to send home with the children and also provide a few recipes they may be able to cook in the classroom as a future project. You may suggest books, field trips or activities that would complement what you introduced in a cooking class.
- Ask the teacher to assist during the cooking demonstration or class, and give him/her a clear role, even if it's just to connect the cooking class with things the students have been studying.
- If you feel like you'll need extra help, ask the teacher to recruit a parent or community member to help during the cooking class or call ASAP and ask us to help recruit a volunteer.

CHAPTER EIGHTEEN

Food Safety

General Food Safety Tips

- Explain safety rules: Begin by explaining safety rules for the cooking class, such as how to use utensils properly, how to turn off the stove and oven, and how to be careful around hot surfaces.
- Use safe tools: Make sure the tools and equipment being used in the cooking class are age-appropriate and safe for children to handle. Avoid using sharp knives, hot surfaces, or other dangerous tools.
- Supervision: Always supervise children closely during the cooking class. An adult should always be present and actively engaged with the children. Never leave children unattended in the kitchen.
- Wash hands: Make sure everyone in the class washes their hands before beginning to cook. This will help prevent the spread of germs and bacteria.
- Proper attire: Encourage students to wear appropriate clothing, such as an apron, to protect their clothes from spills and stains. Tie long hair back to prevent it from getting caught in equipment.

- Stay organized: Keep the cooking area clean and organized to prevent accidents. Make sure the area is free from clutter, spills, and other hazards.
- Be prepared for emergencies: Have a first aid kit on hand and know how to use it. Know where the fire extinguisher is located and how to use it in case of a fire. Make sure there is a clear path to the exit in case of an emergency.
- By following these guidelines, you can help ensure that cooking with children is a safe and enjoyable experience for everyone involved.

Here are a few additional ideas about how to keep your students safe:

1. To prevent food poisoning:

- *Always wash and dry hands thoroughly before cooking.*
- *Do not eat raw eggs.*
- *Wait until the food is cooked before sampling it. Do not sample uncooked foods.*
- *Always wash cutting boards before and after use.*

2. Work with the chef to create a setup that is safe and appropriate for the children. Bring in small tables if necessary where the children can stand or kneel. Always use secure stools or chairs.

3. Tie back long hair.

4. Expect spills and messes, and clean up spills as they happen. Bring extra hand towels or paper towels to handle messes. If you expect something to be particularly messy (e.g., grating beets) make sure to bring plastic or something to protect classroom carpet and tables.

5. Keep handles of pans, pots, etc. pointed towards the center of the stove. If you are using a hot plate, keep handles pointed toward the middle of the table or counter. This will prevent the children from bumping the handle and knocking the pot off the stove.

6. If the children are using knives, the chef should teach them how to hold and handle the knives properly. Be sure an adult is closely supervising children using knives.

7. Use supplies that will not break, such as plastic measuring cups and stainless steel bowls.

8. For young children (5 or younger), use plastic knives or butter knives for spreading or cutting soft foods. Young children can use their fingers to break or tear foods rather than cutting them with a knife, and choppers are also an effective tool for this age group.

9. Provide constant supervision.

- *Always watch students closely when they use knives, mixers, or other equipment.*
- *Closely supervise the use of ovens, stoves, and other kitchen appliances.*
- *Remind children that stoves, ovens, pans, and dishes can be very hot.*

CHAPTER NINETEEN

Safe Food Handling

Before

- If possible, arrange to use the school cafeteria. It will provide more room for the students and is easier to clean before and after the cooking demo.
- Wipe down cooking surfaces, sinks, and prep areas with a bleach solution of one part bleach to 10 parts water. Carefully pour bleach into a spray bottle and then add water. Discard any unused solution after the demo; bleach loses disinfectant power quickly when exposed to heat and sunlight. It's best to mix a new solution each time you use it.
- Allow surfaces to air dry before using them.
- Try to avoid cutting up fresh fruit and veggies until you are ready to use them. If you must prepare items ahead of time, refrigerate them until it is time to use them.
- If harvesting items from the school garden to be cooked, students and staff should wash their hands thoroughly in warm, soapy water for at least 20 seconds.
- If you cook items ahead of time (rice, potatoes, etc.) keep them refrigerated until they are ready to be used.

During

- Instruct students to wash their hands with warm, soapy water before handling food. Hands should be washed for at least 20 seconds (the length of the alphabet song or two rounds of the birthday song).
- Use hand sanitizer after washing if desired, but not as a replacement for washing.
- Wash produce thoroughly before use.
- Instruct students to not touch their hair, face, or clothes after they wash their hands.
- Use caution with raw eggs. Break eggs into a separate container and ensure that there are no shell fragments present. Cook dishes containing eggs thoroughly.

After

- Refrigerate any cooked or cut up foods within two hours.
- Wash cooking equipment and dishes and allow to air dry. Store cooking supplies in a separate cabinet from any chemicals or cleaning supplies.

CHAPTER TWENTY

Knife Safety Tips

When working with knives in a cooking class, it's important to ensure that students are aware of the risks involved and understand how to handle knives safely. Here are some tips to help you teach knife safety:

- Always use a cutting board: Make sure students use a cutting board when cutting ingredients, rather than holding the ingredient in their hand.
- Hold the knife properly: The knife should be held with the thumb and index finger on the handle, and the other three fingers wrapped around the handle. The hand holding the food should be in a "claw" shape to keep fingers away from the blade.

- Keep the blade pointed away: When not in use, the knife should be pointed away from the body.
- Cut away from the body: Always cut away from the body to avoid accidental cuts.
- Keep fingers clear: Fingers should be kept clear of the blade at all times.
- Use a sawing motion: When cutting, use a sawing motion rather than a chopping motion. This will help prevent the knife from slipping and causing injury.

- Sharpen knives regularly: Dull knives are more dangerous than sharp knives, as they require more force to cut and are more likely to slip.

In addition to these tips, it's important to ensure that students understand the school's knife policy and use appropriate tools for their age and skill level. By taking the time to teach knife safety, you can help ensure that your cooking class is a safe and enjoyable experience for everyone involved.

Remember:

- Always cut with the blade of the knife angled down and away from you. Sometimes this is a hard rule to follow. If the angle is wrong, the kids may need you to turn the product around or turn the cutting board around. (Demonstrate this.)
- Always use a cutting board. Never cut anything that is placed in your hand, and do not cut something while holding it up in the air, as there is a greater chance of cutting yourself without a stable surface. Use the board and make sure it has ample space for the task. If your cutting board doesn't have rubber feet, keep it firmly in place by planting a damp towel or paper towel underneath to keep it from moving around the countertop.
- Show children how to hold knives properly with the fingers of their dominant hand securely gripping the knife handle and the fingers of their other hand curled under as they hold the food.
- Never, ever grab a falling knife. The best way to avoid a knife falling is to make sure your knife is always completely on your work surface, without the handle

sticking out into traffic areas.

- Keep knives on the table, and never carry them around the room.
- When you have a knife in hand, keep your eyes on the blade. Nine times out of ten, when people cut themselves they do so when they are looking away from what they are cutting. The simple fact is: you're unlikely to cut yourself if you're watching the blade, especially the tip.
- Make a flat surface on round objects. Before getting started, demonstrate how to make a flat surface on an object prior to cutting. If the child is young, cut the object yourself and create a flat surface before they begin. For example, a round tomato will be likely to roll and will be difficult for a child to cut. If you cut off the top or bottom to create a flat surface, the child will be able to easily handle and cut the tomato safely.
- Remember: graters, zesters, and peelers are sharp too. Warn kids that they are sharp and show them how to properly hold the equipment before they get started.
- Hand-wash your knives and dry thoroughly. Never put knives into the dishwasher or drop them into a sink filled with sudsy water.

CHAPTER TWENTY-ONE

Cooking Equipment

Recommended Cooking Equipment:

1. Large and small cutting boards
2. Saucepans and large cooking pots
3. Induction burner
4. Colander
5. Mixing bowls
6. Measuring cups
7. Measuring spoons
8. Choppers
9. Graters
10. Peelers
11. Apple slicers
12. Serrated knives
13. Paring knives
14. Plastic knives
15. Garlic press
16. Tongs
17. Metal spoons
18. Whisk
19. Metal spatula

20. Rubber spatula
21. Masher
22. Ladle
23. Funnel
24. Tasting cups
25. Napkins, plastic forks, spoons, paper plates and bowls
26. Apple Corer/peeler
27. Extension cord

Equipments Explained:

1. Large and small cutting boards: Cutting boards are essential tools for food preparation. They provide a flat and stable surface for chopping, dicing, and slicing fruits, vegetables, and meats. Having both large and small cutting boards ensures that different sizes of ingredients can be chopped and prepared as needed.
2. Saucepans and large cooking pots: These are essential for boiling, simmering, and cooking large amounts of food. They come in different sizes to suit different cooking needs.
3. Induction burner: An induction burner is a portable cook-top that uses magnetic fields to generate heat. It is useful when you need an extra cooking surface, or you don't have access to a stove.
4. Colander: A colander is a strainer that is used to drain water from cooked or washed ingredients such as pasta, vegetables, or fruits.
5. Mixing bowls: Mixing bowls are used for mixing ingredients together before cooking. They come in different sizes and materials such as stainless steel, glass,

or plastic.

6. Measuring cups: Measuring cups are used to measure liquid ingredients accurately.
7. Measuring spoons: Measuring spoons are used to measure small amounts of ingredients such as salt, baking powder, or spices.
8. Choppers: Choppers are used to chop vegetables, nuts, or fruits into small pieces.
9. Graters: Graters are used to grate cheese, vegetables, or fruits.
10. Peelers: Peelers are used to remove the outer layer of vegetables and fruits such as potatoes, carrots, or apples.
11. Apple slicers: Apple slicers are used to cut apples into wedges or slices.
12. Serrated knives: Serrated knives are used for cutting through bread, tomatoes, and other foods with a tough exterior and a soft interior.
13. Paring knives: Paring knives are used for peeling and trimming vegetables and fruits.
14. Plastic knives: Plastic knives are safe for children to use and are suitable for cutting soft ingredients such as cheese or cooked vegetables.
15. Garlic press: A garlic press is used to crush garlic into a paste-like consistency.
16. Tongs: Tongs are used for flipping, turning, or grabbing food such as meat or vegetables.
17. Metal spoons: Metal spoons are used for stirring, mixing, or serving food.
18. Whisk: A whisk is used for beating eggs, mixing ingredients, or incorporating air into a mixture.
19. Metal spatula: A metal spatula is used for flipping or transferring food such as pancakes, eggs, or hamburgers.

20. Rubber spatula: A rubber spatula is used for scraping the sides of mixing bowls or transferring mixtures from one container to another.
21. Masher: A masher is used for mashing boiled potatoes or other vegetables.
22. Ladle: A ladle is used for serving soup, stew, or other liquids.
23. Funnel: A funnel is used for transferring liquids or dry ingredients into a container with a narrow opening.
24. Tasting cups: Tasting cups are used for sampling or tasting small portions of food.
25. Napkins, plastic forks, spoons, paper plates and bowls: These items are used for serving and eating food.
26. Apple Corer/peeler: An apple corer/peeler is used to remove the core and peel apples.
27. Extension cord: An extension cord is used to provide extra power outlets when cooking appliances need to be plugged in but are too far away from the power source.

And Not to Forget:

When organizing a cooking class, we suggest packing enough tools for the entire class. This means bringing six or seven bowls rather than one, ten or twelve knives rather than two, etc. The equipment you need will depend on the recipe you are making with the students. However, for all of the cooking demos, we also suggest bringing the following, must-have items:

- Paper towels/clean dish towels
- Paper plates/sample cups
- Paper cups
- Plastic disposable gloves
- Hand sanitizer

CHAPTER TWENTY-TWO

Connecting Cooking with Curriculum

Learning Integration: Connecting Cooking with Curriculum

There are many ways to bring curriculum into cooking in the classroom! You can use these objectives as a starting point for brainstorming how to integrate grade level goals into cooking activities.

English Language Arts

- Introduce new vocabulary words to students that are relevant to the recipe.
- Describe how ingredients smell, look, or taste using descriptive adjectives.
- Read and decipher a recipe.
- Write a review of the completed recipe.
- Listen actively to the recipe steps as they are explained by the teacher or chef.
- Look up a recipe for an item growing in the school garden.
- Write, compile and illustrate a collection of recipes.

- Read a book about cooking or growing the main ingredient.
- Write a letter to the farmer who grew the main ingredient for the recipe.
- Create a creative, rhyming name for the completed recipe.
- Research the main ingredient. Make sure to decipher between facts and opinions!
- Interview a grandparent about their favorite foods and recipes when they were young.

Healthful Living

- Discuss proper hand washing techniques before cooking or eating.
- Determine the food groups for each ingredient of the recipe.
- Visit the school garden or look at photos to see examples of the ingredient growing.
- Wait for all students to be served before tasting the finished recipe.
- Discuss the safe use of knives and methods to prevent injury.
- Share a food item equally with a partner.
- Write and discuss rules for cooking as a class or in small groups.
- Choose an item of food, research and report on its path from production through processing to consumption.

Mathematics

- Compare quantities, sizes, weights, volume, or mass of ingredients.
- Sort ingredients by color or shape.
- Divide fruits and vegetables into equal sized pieces.
- Double or triple the ingredients in a recipe to make a larger quantity.
- Use nonstandard measurement to measure the ingredients or objects in the classroom. How many apples high are the students?

Science

- Introduce students to cooking tools and units of measure.
- Observe the properties of liquids. What happens when students combine oil and vinegar for a salad dressing?
- Observe the changes of state when an ingredient is heated, cooled, or mixed with another ingredient.
- What might happen if the unit of measurement was changed?

Social Studies

- Highlight recipes and ingredients that are unique to a particular culture.

- Share traditional family recipes that have been passed down among generations.
- Set up a market in the classroom and "purchase" or barter for ingredients.
- Discuss the history of common foods, food preservation techniques, and storage crops. What items are traditionally produced in North Carolina?
- Sample several different types of something (herbs, varieties of apples, etc.) and vote on a favorite.
- Report on the background of specific ethnic foods – where they come from, how they are grown, and how they are used.

CHAPTER TWENTY-THREE

Journaling with a Cooking Class

Cooking with students presents dozens of opportunities for journaling. Give students time to write in their journals before and after the cooking class, asking them to predict something about the cooking class or reflect on what they have cooked or experienced. With successful journal prompts, you can help them get the very most from the hands-on cooking experience. Below we've compiled 10 journal prompts and activities that will get your students thinking creatively. We encourage you to create your own prompts directly related to the recipe you are cooking in your classroom.

Writing Prompts for Cooking Classes

1. What is your favorite vegetable (or fruit)? How does it taste? What does it look like?
2. If you could design your very own pizza/soup/pie, what toppings or ingredients would it have (include at least one vegetable)? How big would it be? Who would eat it?

3. Invent and describe a new fruit that grows on a tree. How big is the tree it grows on? How big is the fruit itself? Cherry size, grapefruit size or even bigger (or smaller)? What does it taste like? When is it ripe? Winter, fall, spring, summer?
4. Invent and describe a vegetable with super powers. Does it make you have x-ray vision? Does it make you fly? What color is it? Where does it grow?
5. Imagine you are a farmer. What would you grow? Where would you live and what tools would you need?
6. Read a children's book that features a local vegetable or fruit that you are cooking with. Ask your students to imagine they are that fruit or vegetable in a garden. Where would you grow? What would you need to live? What other vegetables or fruits would be around you?
7. After the cooking class, write the ingredients of the recipe on the board. Is there any ingredient the students would add more of or take out? Ask the students to re-write the recipe with a change of their own and describe why they would make the change.
8. After the cooking class, ask your students to work in groups and write out the steps of the recipe they learned. Ask them to make a list of each group members' favorite step in the recipe. For younger grades, students can draw a picture of the step they enjoyed the most.
9. Bring several cooking tools to class. Show them to the students and pass them around the room. In their journals, ask the students to first predict how the tool is used in cooking and then to invent a new use for the tool. Younger students can draw the tool being used or you can lead the class in a group discussion on about the tools.

10. If you are cooking with apples show students a whole apple and a piece of dried apple and ask them to describe how each appears. Ask them to predict how the fresh and dried apple will taste. Give them each a bit of the farm fresh apple and dried apple to eat. Guide the students in eating the apple slowly, ask them to smell it and really look at the apple slice before they eat it. Ask them to hold it in their mouths before they chew and swallow it, paying attention to how it feels or tastes. In their journals, ask the students to list descriptive words for the fresh apple and the dried apple. Older students can predict how the apple was dried. What tools were used? How long to they imagine it took for the apple to dry? Minutes? Hours? Weeks?!

CHAPTER TWENTY-FOUR

Recipes for Children by Chef Fulbaria

(The recipes are a contribution from Chef Paresh Fulbaria)

Chef Paresh Fulbaria

About Chef Paresh Fulbaria:

Chef Paresh Fulbaria is a seasoned culinary professional with over two decades of experience in the food and hospitality industry. He is an alumnus of the prestigious Institute of Hotel Management in Ahmedabad, India, where he honed his skills in the art of cooking and culinary management. With a passion for cooking that began at a young age, Chef Fulbaria has since dedicated his career to exploring the world of food and creating culinary delights for others to enjoy.

Throughout his career, Chef Fulbaria has held various positions as an executive chef on merchant ships. He has spent the last 16 years working in this capacity, traveling to all habitable continents of the world and gaining invaluable experience in international cuisine. As an executive chef, he has been responsible for managing all aspects of the ship's kitchen, including menu planning, food preparation, and staff management.

Chef Fulbaria's extensive travels and exposure to different cultures have influenced his cooking style, which blends traditional techniques and flavors from around the world. He has a keen interest in using fresh, local ingredients to create dishes that are not only delicious but also healthy and sustainable. His dedication to his craft and commitment to quality has earned him a reputation as a talented and respected chef in the industry.

Overall, Chef Paresh Fulbaria's experience and expertise in the culinary world make him a valuable asset to any food and hospitality organization. His passion for cooking, combined with his global perspective and commitment to quality, ensures that he is always at the forefront of the industry, creating innovative and exciting dishes that leave a lasting impression on his guests.

(This chapter contains a few sample recipes from Chef Paresh, ranging from appetizers to main courses and from soups to desserts. These recipes cover a range of cuisines including Italian, Chinese, Spanish, Indian, and American. Each recipe provides step-by-step instructions on how to prepare the dish and lists the required ingredients. Whether you are a beginner or an experienced cook, these recipes are easy to follow and can be adapted to your own taste preferences. From comforting classics like mashed potatoes and grilled cheese sandwiches to more adventurous dishes like Chinese fried rice and Spanish omelets, there is something for everyone to enjoy. So, put on your apron, grab your ingredients, and let's start cooking!)

TOMATO SOUP:

Ingredients:

- 1 tablespoon olive oil
- 1 medium onion, chopped
- 2 cloves garlic, minced
- 4 cups fresh tomatoes, chopped
- 2 cups chicken or vegetable broth
- 1 teaspoon dried basil
- Salt and pepper to taste
- 1/2 cup heavy cream (optional)

Instructions:

1. Heat the olive oil in a large pot over medium heat.
2. Add the chopped onion and minced garlic, and sauté until the onion is translucent and the garlic is fragrant.
3. Add the chopped tomatoes and cook for a few minutes until they begin to soften.
4. Add the chicken or vegetable broth, dried basil, salt, and pepper.
5. Bring the mixture to a boil, then reduce the heat and simmer for 20-25 minutes.
6. Allow the soup to cool slightly, then blend it in a blender until smooth.
7. Return the blended soup to the pot, and stir in the heavy cream (if using).

8. Heat the soup until warmed through, and serve hot.
9. Enjoy your delicious and healthy tomato soup!

HOT AND SOUR SOUP:

Ingredients:

- 4 cups chicken or vegetable broth
- 1 cup shiitake mushrooms, sliced
- 1/4 cup bamboo shoots, sliced
- 1/4 cup soy sauce
- 1/4 cup rice vinegar
- 1 tablespoon chili garlic sauce
- 1 tablespoon sesame oil
- 1/4 cup cornstarch
- 1/4 cup water
- 2 eggs, beaten
- 1 cup firm tofu, cubed
- 1/4 cup green onions, sliced
- Salt and pepper, to taste

Instructions:

1. In a large pot, bring the chicken or vegetable broth to a boil.
2. Add in the sliced shiitake mushrooms and bamboo shoots. Let it simmer for 5 minutes.
3. Add soy sauce, rice vinegar, chili garlic sauce, and sesame oil to the pot. Mix well.
4. In a small bowl, mix cornstarch and water until there are no lumps. Slowly pour the cornstarch mixture into the pot, while stirring continuously.
5. Once the soup starts to thicken, add in the beaten eggs and stir until the eggs are cooked.

6. Add in the cubed tofu and green onions. Season with salt and pepper to taste.
7. Let the soup simmer for another 5-10 minutes.
8. Serve hot and enjoy!

SWEET CORN SOUP:
Ingredients:

- 2 cups fresh or frozen sweet corn kernels
- 4 cups vegetable broth
- 2 tablespoons butter
- 1 small onion, chopped
- 1 garlic clove, minced
- 1 teaspoon grated fresh ginger
- 2 tablespoons all-purpose flour
- 1/2 cup heavy cream
- Salt and pepper, to taste
- Chopped fresh cilantro or parsley, for garnish

Instructions:

1. In a blender or food processor, puree 1 cup of the sweet corn with 1 cup of the vegetable broth until smooth. Set aside.
2. In a large pot or Dutch oven, melt the butter over medium heat. Add the onion and garlic, and cook until soft and translucent, about 5 minutes.
3. Add the ginger and remaining sweet corn kernels to the pot, and cook for another 5 minutes, stirring occasionally.
4. Sprinkle the flour over the vegetables and stir to combine. Cook for 1-2 minutes until the flour is lightly browned and fragrant.

5. Gradually whisk in the remaining vegetable broth and the sweet corn puree, and bring to a boil. Reduce the heat and simmer for 10-15 minutes, stirring occasionally, until the soup thickens slightly and the vegetables are tender.
6. Stir in the heavy cream and season with salt and pepper to taste. Heat the soup for another 1-2 minutes until hot, but do not boil.
7. Serve hot, garnished with chopped cilantro or parsley if desired.
8. Enjoy your delicious Sweet Corn Soup!

MASHED POTATOES:

Ingredients:

- 2 pounds potatoes (russet or Yukon gold)
- 1/2 cup milk
- 1/4 cup butter
- Salt
- Pepper

Instructions:

1. Peel the potatoes and cut them into 1-inch cubes. Place them in a large pot and cover with cold water. Add a pinch of salt and bring to a boil.
2. Reduce the heat to medium-low and simmer until the potatoes are tender when pierced with a fork, about 15-20 minutes.
3. Drain the potatoes and return them to the pot.
4. Add the milk and butter to the pot and use a potato masher or a fork to mash the potatoes until smooth. If the potatoes seem too dry, add a little more milk until

they reach your desired consistency.

5. Season with salt and pepper to taste.
6. Serve immediately, garnished with fresh herbs if desired. Enjoy your delicious and creamy mashed potatoes!

FRENCH FRIES:
Ingredients:

- 4 large potatoes
- Vegetable oil
- Salt

Instructions:

1. Peel the potatoes and cut them into evenly sized sticks. Rinse the sticks under cold water to remove excess starch, then dry them thoroughly with a paper towel.
2. Heat the oil in a deep fryer or a heavy-bottomed pot over medium-high heat until it reaches 375°F (190°C).
3. Carefully add a handful of potato sticks to the oil and fry for 2-3 minutes or until they're golden brown and crispy. Use a slotted spoon to remove the fries from the oil and transfer them to a paper towel-lined plate to drain any excess oil.
4. Repeat the frying process with the remaining potato sticks in small batches to avoid overcrowding the pot.
5. Once all the fries are fried, season them with salt to taste and serve hot.

Note: You can also bake the fries in the oven instead of frying them. Preheat your oven to 425°F (218°C) and spread the potato sticks in a single layer on a baking sheet.

Drizzle some vegetable oil over the fries and season them with salt, then bake for 25-30 minutes or until they're crispy and golden brown.

SPAGHETTI CARBONARA:

Ingredients:

- 1 pound spaghetti
- 8 ounces pancetta or bacon, diced
- 4 cloves garlic, minced
- 4 large eggs
- 1 cup grated Parmesan cheese
- 1 cup grated Pecorino Romano cheese
- 1/2 teaspoon black pepper
- Salt to taste

Instructions:

1. Bring a large pot of salted water to a boil. Add the spaghetti and cook until al dente according to package instructions.
2. While the pasta is cooking, heat a large skillet over medium heat. Add the pancetta or bacon and cook until crispy, about 5-7 minutes. Add the garlic and cook for an additional minute.
3. In a bowl, whisk together the eggs, Parmesan cheese, Pecorino Romano cheese, black pepper, and salt.
4. When the spaghetti is done cooking, reserve 1 cup of the pasta water and then drain the spaghetti.
5. Add the spaghetti to the skillet with the pancetta or bacon and toss to combine.
6. Remove the skillet from the heat and pour the egg and cheese mixture over the spaghetti, stirring quickly to coat the pasta evenly. If the sauce seems too thick, add a

splash or two of the reserved pasta water.

7. Serve the pasta immediately, garnished with additional grated Parmesan cheese and black pepper if desired.
8. Enjoy your delicious Italian spaghetti carbonara!

VEGETABLE PIZZA:

Ingredients:

- 1 pre-made pizza crust
- 1/2 cup tomato sauce
- 1 cup shredded mozzarella cheese
- 1/2 cup sliced mushrooms
- 1/2 cup sliced bell peppers
- 1/2 cup sliced onions
- 1/4 cup sliced black olives
- 1/4 cup chopped fresh basil
- 1 tablespoon olive oil

Instructions:

1. Preheat the oven to 450°F.
2. Place the pizza crust on a baking sheet.
3. Spread the tomato sauce evenly over the crust, leaving a small border around the edge.
4. Sprinkle the shredded mozzarella cheese over the tomato sauce.
5. Arrange the sliced mushrooms, bell peppers, onions, and black olives over the cheese.
6. Drizzle the olive oil over the vegetables.
7. Bake the pizza in the preheated oven for 10-15 minutes or until the crust is golden brown and the cheese is melted and bubbly.

8. Remove the pizza from the oven and sprinkle the chopped fresh basil over the top.
9. Slice and serve hot.
10. Enjoy your delicious veg pizza!

MCDONALD'S-STYLE BURGER:

Ingredients:

- 1 pound ground beef (80% lean, 20% fat)
- 4 hamburger buns
- 4 slices American cheese
- 1/4 cup diced onions
- 8 dill pickle slices
- Ketchup
- Mustard
- Salt
- Pepper

Instructions:

1. Preheat a grill or skillet to medium-high heat.
2. Divide the ground beef into 4 equal portions and shape them into patties. Season each patty with salt and pepper.
3. Cook the patties for 3-4 minutes on each side, or until they reach your desired level of doneness.
4. While the patties are cooking, slice the buns in half and lightly toast them.
5. Assemble the burgers by placing a slice of American cheese on the bottom bun, followed by the cooked patty, diced onions, and pickle slices.
6. Spread ketchup and mustard on the top bun, then place it on top of the burger.

7. Serve hot and enjoy your McDonald's-style burger!

CHINESE FIRED RICE:
Ingredients:

- 1 cup of uncooked rice
- 2 cups of water
- 2 tablespoons of oil
- 2 eggs, lightly beaten
- 2 cloves of garlic, minced
- 1/2 cup of frozen peas and carrots, thawed
- 1/2 cup of chopped onion
- 1/4 cup of soy sauce
- Salt and pepper to taste
- Green onions, sliced for garnish

Instructions:

1. Rinse the rice until the water runs clear. Add the rice and water to a medium saucepan and bring to a boil. Reduce heat to low, cover and simmer for 18-20 minutes until the rice is cooked.
2. In a large skillet or wok, heat 1 tablespoon of oil over medium-high heat. Add the beaten eggs and scramble until they are fully cooked. Remove the eggs from the skillet and set them aside.
3. Add the remaining tablespoon of oil to the same skillet or wok. Add the minced garlic, chopped onion, peas and carrots, and cook for 2-3 minutes until the vegetables are tender.
4. Add the cooked rice and scrambled eggs to the skillet or wok, and stir until well combined.

5. Pour the soy sauce over the rice and egg mixture, and stir until the rice is evenly coated.
6. Season with salt and pepper to taste. Cook for another 2-3 minutes until everything is heated through.
7. Serve the fried rice hot, garnished with sliced green onions if desired. Enjoy!

GRILLED SANDWICH:

Ingredients:

- 4 slices of bread
- 2 tbsp butter, softened
- 4 slices of cheese
- 4 slices of cooked ham or turkey
- 1/2 small onion, sliced
- 1 small tomato, sliced
- Salt and pepper to taste

Instructions:

1. Preheat a sandwich maker or grill pan.
2. Spread softened butter on one side of each slice of bread.
3. Place one slice of bread, buttered side down, on the sandwich maker or grill pan.
4. Place a slice of cheese on top of the bread, followed by a slice of ham or turkey, onion slices, tomato slices, salt, and pepper.
5. Place another slice of cheese on top of the vegetables, followed by another slice of bread, buttered side up.
6. Close the sandwich maker or grill pan and cook until the cheese is melted and the bread is golden brown, about 5-6 minutes.

7. Repeat with the remaining bread and ingredients to make the second sandwich.
8. Cut each sandwich in half and serve hot. Enjoy!

STUFFED PARATHA:
Ingredients:

- 2 cups whole wheat flour
- 1 tsp salt
- 1 tsp red chilli powder
- 1/2 tsp turmeric powder
- 1/2 tsp cumin powder
- 1/2 tsp coriander powder
- 2 tbsp oil
- Water as needed
- Oil or ghee for cooking
- Filling of your choice (potatoes, cauliflower, paneer, etc.)

Instructions:

1. In a large mixing bowl, add the whole wheat flour, salt, red chilli powder, turmeric powder, cumin powder, coriander powder, and oil. Mix well.
2. Add water little by little and knead the dough until it becomes soft and pliable. Cover and let the dough rest for 15-20 minutes.
3. Meanwhile, prepare the filling of your choice. You can use potatoes, cauliflower, paneer, or any other vegetable of your choice. Cook the vegetables until they are soft and mashable. Add salt, red chilli powder, garam masala, and chopped coriander leaves for flavor.

4. Divide the dough into small balls. Roll each ball into a small circle and place a spoonful of the filling in the center.
5. Fold the edges of the circle towards the center, covering the filling completely. Roll the stuffed ball into a larger circle, taking care not to let the filling come out.
6. Heat a tawa or a flat pan. Place the stuffed paratha on the tawa and cook on medium heat until brown spots appear on both sides.
7. Apply oil or ghee on both sides and cook until the paratha is crispy and golden brown.
8. Serve hot with yogurt, chutney, or pickle.

MUFFINS:

Ingredients:

- 1 and 1/2 cups of all-purpose flour
- 1/2 cup of granulated sugar
- 2 teaspoons of baking powder
- 1/4 teaspoon of salt
- 1/2 cup of unsalted butter, melted and cooled
- 1/2 cup of whole milk
- 2 large eggs
- 1 teaspoon of vanilla extract
- 1/2 cup of semi-sweet chocolate chips

Instructions:

1. Preheat the oven to 375°F (190°C) and line a 12-cup muffin pan with paper liners.
2. In a large mixing bowl, whisk together the flour, sugar, baking powder, and salt.

3. In a separate mixing bowl, whisk together the melted butter, whole milk, eggs, and vanilla extract until well combined.
4. Pour the wet ingredients into the dry ingredients and stir until just combined.
5. Fold in the chocolate chips.
6. Divide the batter evenly among the 12 muffin cups.
7. Bake for 18-20 minutes or until a toothpick inserted into the center of a muffin comes out clean.
8. Remove the muffins from the oven and let cool in the pan for 5 minutes before transferring to a wire rack to cool completely.
9. Enjoy your delicious Vanilla Chocolate Muffins!

MILK PUDDING:

Ingredients:

- 4 cups milk
- 3 tbsp cornstarch
- 1/2 cup sugar
- 1 tsp vanilla extract
- 1/4 tsp ground cinnamon (optional)

Instructions:

1. In a large saucepan, whisk together the cornstarch and sugar.
2. Gradually whisk in the milk until no lumps remain.
3. Heat the mixture over medium heat, stirring constantly, until it comes to a simmer and begins to thicken, about 8-10 minutes.

4. Once thickened, remove the pan from the heat and stir in the vanilla extract and ground cinnamon, if using.
5. Pour the mixture into individual serving cups or a large bowl.
6. Allow the pudding to cool to room temperature before refrigerating for at least 1-2 hours, or until completely chilled and set.
7. Serve cold, optionally topped with whipped cream, fresh fruit, or chocolate shavings.

KHEER (a popular Indian rice pudding):
Ingredients:

- 1/2 cup basmati rice
- 4 cups whole milk
- 1/2 cup sugar
- 1/2 tsp ground cardamom
- 2 tbsp chopped almonds
- 2 tbsp chopped pistachios
- 1 tbsp golden raisins
- 1 tbsp ghee (clarified butter)
- Pinch of saffron strands

Instructions:

1. Wash the rice thoroughly in water and soak for 20 minutes. Drain the water and set aside.
2. Heat the ghee in a heavy-bottomed pan on medium heat.
3. Add the soaked rice and sauté for 2-3 minutes until the rice turns translucent.
4. Add the whole milk and bring it to a boil on medium heat. Reduce the heat to low and let the rice cook for

about 25-30 minutes or until it softens, stirring occasionally to prevent sticking.

5. Add the sugar, cardamom powder, and saffron to the pan and mix well.
6. Continue to cook on low heat until the kheer thickens to your desired consistency, stirring frequently.
7. Add the chopped almonds, pistachios, and raisins to the kheer and mix well.
8. Turn off the heat and let the kheer cool down to room temperature.
9. Once cooled, refrigerate the kheer for at least 2 hours before serving.
10. Serve chilled or at room temperature, garnished with additional chopped nuts, if desired. Enjoy!

SOOJI KA HALWA (Semolina Pudding):
Ingredients:

- 1 cup semolina (sooji/rava)
- 1/2 cup ghee (clarified butter)
- 1 cup sugar
- 3 cups water
- 1/4 cup chopped cashews
- 1/4 cup raisins
- 1/4 tsp cardamom powder
- A few strands of saffron (optional)

Instructions:

1. Heat a heavy-bottomed pan on medium heat and add ghee to it. Once the ghee melts, add the semolina and roast it until it turns golden brown and gives off a nutty aroma.

2. In another pot, add water and sugar and heat it on medium heat until the sugar dissolves. Turn off the heat and keep the sugar syrup aside.
3. Once the semolina is roasted, add the chopped cashews and raisins and mix well.
4. Add the sugar syrup to the semolina mixture slowly, while stirring continuously to avoid lumps.
5. Add the cardamom powder and saffron strands (if using) and mix well.
6. Reduce the heat to low and cover the pan with a lid. Let it cook for 5-7 minutes, stirring occasionally until the halwa thickens and the ghee starts to separate from the mixture.
7. Once the halwa reaches the desired consistency, turn off the heat and let it rest for a few minutes before serving.
8. Garnish with some more chopped cashews and serve hot.
9. Enjoy your delicious Sooji ka Halwa!

SPANISH OMELET:
Ingredients:

- 3 large eggs
- 1 medium potato
- 1/2 small onion, chopped
- 1/2 red bell pepper, chopped
- 2 tablespoons olive oil
- Salt and pepper to taste

Instructions:

1. Peel and thinly slice the potato into rounds.

2. In a non-stick skillet over medium heat, add 1 tablespoon of olive oil and the potato slices. Cook for 8-10 minutes or until tender and golden brown.
3. Add the chopped onion and red bell pepper to the skillet and cook for another 3-4 minutes until softened.
4. In a mixing bowl, beat the eggs with salt and pepper until fully mixed.
5. Add the cooked potatoes, onion, and red bell pepper to the bowl with the eggs and mix well.
6. Heat 1 tablespoon of olive oil in the same skillet used to cook the vegetables over medium heat.
7. Pour the egg mixture into the skillet and cook for 5-7 minutes or until the edges start to set.
8. Place a plate over the skillet and carefully flip the omelet onto the plate.
9. Slide the omelet back into the skillet with the uncooked side facing down.
10. Cook for another 2-3 minutes until fully set.
11. Slide the omelet onto a plate, slice and serve hot.

FISH CUTLET:

Ingredients:

- 500g boneless fish (any white fish like cod or haddock)
- 1 large onion, chopped
- 2-3 green chilies, chopped
- 1/4 cup chopped fresh coriander leaves
- 1/4 tsp turmeric powder
- 1 tsp red chili powder
- 1 tsp coriander powder
- 1 tsp cumin powder
- 1 tsp garam masala powder
- 1 tsp lemon juice

- Salt, to taste
- 2-3 slices of bread, crumbled
- 2 eggs, beaten
- Oil, for frying

Instructions:

1. Boil the fish in water until it is cooked and tender. Drain and set aside to cool.
2. Once the fish is cool enough to handle, use your fingers to flake it into small pieces.
3. In a large bowl, mix together the fish, onion, green chilies, coriander leaves, turmeric powder, red chili powder, coriander powder, cumin powder, garam masala powder, lemon juice and salt.
4. Add the crumbled bread and beaten eggs to the mixture and mix well.
5. Using your hands, shape the mixture into small patties or cutlets.
6. Heat oil in a frying pan over medium heat.
7. Gently place the cutlets into the hot oil and fry until they are golden brown on both sides.
8. Remove the cutlets from the oil and place them on a paper towel-lined plate to absorb any excess oil.
9. Serve hot with ketchup or any dip of your choice.

CHICKEN CURRY:
Ingredients:

- 500g chicken, cut into small pieces
- 2 onions, finely chopped
- 4 garlic cloves, minced
- 2 tomatoes, chopped

- 2 tbsp vegetable oil
- 1 tsp cumin seeds
- 1 tsp coriander powder
- 1 tsp turmeric powder
- 1 tsp red chili powder
- 1 tsp garam masala powder
- Salt to taste
- Water
- Fresh coriander leaves, chopped

Instructions:

1. Heat the oil in a large pan over medium heat. Add the cumin seeds and let them splutter.
2. Add the chopped onions and sauté until they turn golden brown.
3. Add the minced garlic and sauté for a minute.
4. Add the chopped tomatoes and sauté for 2-3 minutes until they turn soft.
5. Add the chicken pieces and mix well with the onion-tomato mixture.
6. Add the coriander powder, turmeric powder, red chili powder, and salt. Mix well.
7. Add enough water to cover the chicken and bring the mixture to a boil.
8. Cover the pan and let the chicken cook on low-medium heat for 20-25 minutes, or until it is tender and cooked through.
9. Add the garam masala powder and mix well.
10. Garnish with fresh coriander leaves and serve hot with rice or roti.

BOILED RICE:

Ingredients:

- 1 cup rice
- 2 cups water
- Salt (optional)

Instructions:

1. Rinse the rice with cold water in a fine-mesh strainer until the water runs clear.
2. In a medium-sized pot, add the rinsed rice and 2 cups of water. If you want, you can also add a pinch of salt to enhance the flavor.
3. Bring the water to a boil over high heat.
4. Once the water starts boiling, reduce the heat to low and cover the pot with a lid.
5. Allow the rice to simmer for 18-20 minutes, or until the water has been absorbed by the rice and the rice is fully cooked.
6. Turn off the heat and let the rice rest in the covered pot for 5-10 minutes.
7. After 5-10 minutes, uncover the pot and fluff the rice with a fork.
8. The boiled rice is now ready to serve.

GREEN SALAD:
Ingredients:

- 4 cups mixed salad greens
- 1 cucumber, sliced
- 1 avocado, diced
- 1/2 red onion, sliced
- 1/2 cup cherry tomatoes, halved

- 1/4 cup crumbled feta cheese
- 1/4 cup toasted pine nuts
- For the dressing:
- 1/4 cup extra-virgin olive oil
- 2 tablespoons red wine vinegar
- 1 garlic clove, minced
- 1 teaspoon Dijon mustard
- Salt and freshly ground black pepper, to taste

Instructions:

1. Wash and dry the mixed salad greens, and place them in a large bowl.
2. Add the sliced cucumber, diced avocado, sliced red onion, halved cherry tomatoes, and crumbled feta cheese.
3. In a small bowl, whisk together the extra-virgin olive oil, red wine vinegar, minced garlic, and Dijon mustard. Season with salt and freshly ground black pepper, to taste.
4. Pour the dressing over the salad, and toss to combine.
5. Sprinkle the toasted pine nuts over the top of the salad.
6. Serve immediately.

The Author

Dr Anshumali Pandey

Dr. Anshumali Pandey is a name synonymous with excellence in education, hospitality, tourism, and tribal food. A multifaceted personality, he is a teacher, chef, author, business auditor, and culinary traveler. With a specialization in higher education, office administration, HR, labor laws, audit, procurement, and tender processes, Dr. Pandey is a renowned hospitality educator with a PhD.

His passion for tribal food, tourism, and village tourism has led to extensive research in these areas, resulting in several research papers and publications. His expertise has earned him recognition from the Ministry of Tourism, Government of India, which awarded him a National Appreciation certificate and memento in 2018.

Dr. Pandey's vast experience of over 26 years in the professional world has boiled down to crisp and accurate writing on his favorite subjects, resulting in 83 publications, consisting of 65 books and several short stories. His books cover a broad range of topics, from being a specialist chef, a master of human resources, an educator, a children's book author, to spirituality.

Living with his family in the Western Indian tribal belt of the union territory of Dadra & Nagar Haveli for over two decades, Dr. Pandey has dedicated most of his time to helping and understanding the tribal and rural population of the region. His writings are a banquet of his vast expertise, and his knowledge is evident from the spectrum of subjects he has chosen for his books. Dr. Anshumali Pandey is a hospitality sector champion who excels in multiple fields, making him a reliable and renowned name in the industry.

Books written by the Author are –

1. Theory of Indian Cookery
2. Beauty and Irony of Silvassa Tourism
3. A Short Indian Food Story
4. Be Your Own Guide to Indian Cuisine
5. Cookery Fundamentals
6. History of Indian Food (2 Editions Printed)
7. The Great Indian Story Book for Children
8. Personal Budget: Easy Work Book
9. Online Classes Log Book
10. Dictionary Making Work Book for School Children
11. The Lazy Bed
12. Hindu Dharm (हन्दि् धर्म) (In Hindi Language)
13. Where is my coffee?
14. Your First Job is Never your Last (Volume 1)
15. You are Almost There (Quick Fix Resume and Interview Hacks)

16. Working for the Enemy? - A lesson in Career Management
17. Public Speaking for the Young
18. A Date With Coffee
19. How to be The Best Hotel Front Office Employee
20. Diploma in Food Production, The complete Syllabus
21. Diploma in F&B Service, The Complete Syllabus
22. Diploma in Front Office, The Complete Syllabus
23. The Time to Speak is Now
24. Munshi Premchand (Short Stories in English)
25. The Housekeeping Department, Text Book
26. Hitchhiker's Guide to Trekking in Uttarakhand
27. Uttarakhand, A divine Land for a Reason
28. Bachhon ke liye rochak kahaniyan (बच्चों के लिए रोचक कहानियाँ) (In Hindi Language)
29. Basic Communication Skills of English
30. The Basic Office Organisation Book for Start-ups
31. Hospitality HRM
32. Hospitality Marketing
33. Bakery Ingredients and Tools
34. Human Resource Management for Indian Professionals
35. The process of LAWFULLY operating a Hospitality business in India
36. Indian Classical Sweets: History, Tradition and Recipes
37. History of India's Himalayan Cuisine: Classical Cookery of Kashmir, Laddakh, Jammu, Himachal, Lahaul, Spiti, Garhwal, Kumaon.
38. Vindu: Andhra Cuisine (Part 1 of South Indian Trilogy)
39. Saappadu: Tamil Cuisine (Part 2 of South Indian Trilogy)
40. Sadya: Malayali Cuisine (Part 3 of South Indian Trilogy)
41. South Indian Cuisine - The Researcher's Guide Book

42. The Ramayana for Children and other short stories from Indian Mythology
43. Legends of the Tribal Shiva
44. Third Generation Children's Story Book
45. It's Elementary: The Top Nine Adventures from the memoirs of Dr John H Watson
46. UNITY IN DIVERSITY, The foundation of Indian Tourism
47. The Thar Express: Culinary History of Rajasthan and Gujarat
48. Basics of Computerized Accounting
49. Impact (Impact of Globalization on Indian Social Life)
50. Vishnu – The Lord of Amazing Incarnations
51. Being a Mahatma in the Freedom Struggle
52. The Culinary Journey of Purvanchal: Lucknow to Patna
53. Culinary History of the Gangetic Plains
54. Indian Culinary Secrets
55. The Story of Jain and Parsi Food
56. The Great Indian Pilgrimage Tourism
57. Introduction to Tourism Studies – Text Book
58. Bread and Rolls
59. Diploma in Digital Marketing the Complete Syllabus
60. The Theory of Sweetened Bakery Foods
61. Campus Placement Guide for Management Trainee in Leading Hotels
62. Diploma in Housekeeping Management, the Complete Syllabus
63. Jokes and Stories for Kids
64. Demigods of India
65. Practical Cookery Guide Book for Parents and School Teachers

Connect with me: anshumali.pandey@gmail.com

https://notionpress.com/author/337004

Please scan this QR code on your phone to know more about the latest and complete works of Dr Anshumali Pandey

Printed by Libri Plureos GmbH in Hamburg,
Germany